WHAT I LEARNED IN THE STREETS & PRISON

THAT CAN HELP YOU *WIN* AT THE GAME OF LIFE

BY
EDWARD BALL

Published By:

BALLTEAM LLC
ENTERPRISE

©2013 by Edward Ball

All rights reserved. No parts of this publication may
be reproduced, distributed, or transmitted in any
form by any means without the written permission
of the publisher.

eBook ISBN: 978-0-9899864-1-0

Paper back ISBN: 978-0-9899864-3-4

***

TABLE OF CONTENTS

Introduction 1

SECTION I: THE GAME 8

Chapter 1 Charge it to The Game 9

Chapter 2 Roll or Get Rolled Over 15

Chapter 3 Quit Rappin' 22

Chapter 4 Respect the Game 29

Chapter 5 Don't get knocked off your square 34

Chapter 6 Man sharpens man 41

Chapter 7 Do you 46

Chapter 8 Have heart have money 50

Chapter 9 If he aint hungry don't feed him 55

Chapter 10 Stick to the script 59

Chapter 11 Hully Gully 63

Chapter 13 Get your mind right 68

Chapter 12 Pride comes before the fall..................73

Chapter 14 You are only as strong as those under you allow you to be..77

Chapter 15 Talk to the head not the tail.................81

SECTION II: GAME RECOGNIZES GAME...86

Chapter 16 Game recognizes game 87

Chapter 17 Don't be a stepping stone....................93

Chapter 18 Make sure your knife isn't used to do the stabbing..99

Chapter 19 Beware of the Herald's message.......104

Chapter 20 Keep an eye on those who are doing too much 107

Chapter 21 Alternatives used as deception..........112

Chapter 22 Don't focus on the fire 118

Chapter 23 Beware of Ear Hustlers 122

Chapter 24 Watch the moves of those watching your moves..126

Chapter 25 Beware of offers you can't refuse 132

Chapter 26 Everybody plays the fool sometimes 136

Chapter 27 Peep Game: Everything is significant and has meaning 140

Chapter 28 Enemies are close..............................146

Chapter 29 Watch your first step 151

Chapter 30 Pay attention to what's not being said 157

Conclusion 166

About the Author 170

***

Introduction

Game can be defined in several ways. However, there are two definitions of game I find important. The first definition of game is: Game is an occupation or business along with its rules and loopholes. The second definition of game is: Game is a calculated strategy or systematic plan. The fact is we all need to have some type of game to survive. We all need to have game because we are thrust into the ultimate game: the game of life.

Game is a business or occupation and is basically

something we play. Some games have higher stakes than others. Not all games are legitimate. Selling drugs is a game, selling apparel is a game, creating software is a game and chasing men or women is a game.

People in these games and others, either have game or not. In other words they know how to play the game or they don't. If you don't know the rules and loopholes of the particular game you are in you can't successfully play the game. In fact, you really can't play the game at all; all you would be doing is messing up the game.

An accountant has game if he: knows all of the generally accepted accounting principles, the rules of his profession; the laws and the loopholes, helps you make money and decreases your tax burden. He has game because he is in an occupation/business within which he can do his job well. On the other hand if you deal with an accountant who doesn't know the ins and outs, GAAP's, tax law and the loopholes your tax burden may increase and you may even get audited. That accountant has no game, at least in the realm of accounting.

Another form or aspect of game is a calculated strategy or systematic plan. Whenever you approach an endeavor it is imperative to have a strategic plan. Only a person who is without game gets into something all willy-nilly. Something as simple as speaking to a woman requires a plan. The plan may be flexible and tailored to the woman. The plan may include what you are going to say and how you are going to say it. The ability to formulate an effective plan comes from knowing the rules of the game; and there are rules for speaking to men, women and even children. There are rules governing how you speak to certain categories of men, women and children.

CEOs of big and small businesses alike, operate them according to the strategic plan they created. A CEO with game gets in the game of business and makes it profitable. This CEO knows how the game goes or knows the rules, written, unwritten and the loopholes which allow him to create a great strategic plan.

Even crooks use game to separate you from your valuables. First of all, they enter into a particular game of some sort or specific type of crime; then they formulate a scheme to rob you and get away with it. They run game so good you are left in disbelief after you realize you've been had.

In actuality there are so many games to play within this game of life, and even more ways to play them, that you need to constantly be improving your game. This will allow you to be successful at the overall game of life. People with game know the rules of the game(s) and use those rules to their advantage. Since you can't know everything, a person with game should know his shortcomings and find teammates to fill the gaps.

You can be given game. Your parents give you game, so much game you should be winning at the game of life. But you probably didn't listen to the majority of the game you were given. Because you can be given the game, places like school have been created along with programs like apprenticeships and mentoring. In addition, you can get game from books.

In the first part of this book I give tid bits of game I think can play a role in helping you be more successful and perhaps a bit more cynical and suspicious in life. The tid bits in the second half of this book can help you avoid having some, not all, game ran on you. I think many of the bits of game in this book are familiar and most likely have been experienced by you. However, they may have been experienced differently or characterized differently. In any event they will be helpful to you.

If you know the rules of the game, have the ability and willingness to play the game how it goes and have the capacity to think critically and strategically you pretty much have game. You can recognize game when you see it and get in the game and play it successfully.

Game is a tool not a ruler. Rulers use game as a tool

I believe many of you are playing the game buttnaked: You don't have a uniform, a bat, shoes, a glove or teammates and that's why you are losing. As you start peeping game you begin to acquire gloves, bats and uniforms and you start building a team. Equipped with these tools you can play the game the way it was meant and increase your chances at success and avoid being struck out inning after inning. Hopefully this book will allow you to either start peeping game or add another dynamic to your game. You are either at the game or in the game. I want to help you change the game. If you are at the game you are being played, if you are in the game you are doing the playing. By changing the game you make others play by your rules.

I must give my readers a warning. I have spent over 13 straight years in prison. As a result my points of view, beliefs and perspectives may be skewed and way off the mark. However, everything I say is my reality created from my unique experiences.

***

SECTION I: THE GAME

Chapter 1
Charge it to The Game

Often you can get so caught up in an endeavor, person or thing that you can't let it go. You probably have invested so much that you feel it would be a waste not to continue. However, it may be better to cut your losses and move on. This is true for various reasons. First, when you let it go you are taking control. Second, you position yourself to take advantage of other opportunities. Finally, when you "charge it to the game" your focus shifts from what you want it to be, to what it is.

When I am playing a game my goal is to take control of my opponent. One of my tactics is to get out ahead of my adversary. Once I am ahead of him he is chasing me, all that he has lost and everything he has invested. Then I begin doing things to frustrate him. When he becomes frustrated he is no longer thinking clearly. Instead of walking away and charging his losses to the game he chases after them. He is out of control; he can't let it go and before he knows it he has lost everything including the game, his temper and his confidence.

The moment my adversary stops playing and charges his little losses to the game he nullifies my control. Also, he gains control over whether we will continue to play and control over his temper. Now he can get his mind right and play more of a role in determining the outcome of the game or move on to bigger and better things.

What is seen in many relationships are people who refuse to charge it to the game. They stay with their loser girlfriend, wife, boyfriend or husband even after nearly losing everything because of them. They refuse to cut their losses and move on. The result is that they miss out on that good man or woman and stay stuck with a sinking ship. Pimps use this tactic to keep their whores. They make new whores pay to get pimped. The logic is that if the girl gets the idea to leave the pimp she immediately begins to think about all the money and other things she has invested in, and for, this pimp. Seems like it would make more sense to stay with her investment than it would to move on and leave it all behind. Her attachment to things, her investment and her unwillingness to charge it to the game keeps her from gaining her freedom.

In life you can get involved in things that drag you down but because you have put so much time, money, sweat and tears into it, you can't or won't let them go and you miss opportunities. The wise thing to do would be to charge your investment to the game and take advantage of all the opportunities that come your way; opportunities you might otherwise miss while holding on to a sinking ship. At the very least, when you let it go or charge it to the game you are in the right state of mind and position to jump on other opportunities that come your way.

Prior to going to prison I was shot by someone I knew from the neighborhood. I was so caught up in making his life miserable and getting revenge that I couldn't let it go. I wasted some of the best years of my life in prison because I didn't charge it to the game. In addition, I repudiated a support system that would have helped me do anything in the world. However, I was so caught up in what I wanted it to be that I didn't take advantage of what it was.

I should have taken the shooting as a hazard that comes with being in the streets, left it there and moved on. Fighters know that when they enter the ring they can get knocked out. If they do get knocked out they don't go chasing down the guy that knocked them out trying to kill him. Good fighters simply charge it to the game of fighting; they move on, continue to train and keep fighting. When and if they face a fighter again they are better prepared to do the knocking out.

How to win: Have Game

You win by:

1. Taking control

2. Positioning yourself

Life is too short to be chasing what is already lost. You need to take control and let that lost thing go. If you have a hundred dollars and lose ten, you can't spend all day and the remaining 90 dollars trying to find the lost 10. You can miss out on the chance to make a thousand dollars because you are chasing that lost ten. Charge that 10 to the game and position yourself to grasp the opportunities around you.

Your focus needs to go from what you want it to be to what it is. Continuing with our example, what you want it to be is that you find that ten dollars. However, you have 90 dollars and that's what it is. You should focus on the 90 before you lose that too. Some things need to be charged to the game.

***

Chapter 2
Roll or Get Rolled Over

In the processes of handling your business there are a few things that need to take place to increase the likelihood of your success. First, you should part from anyone who hinders you from handling your business. Second, get away from people who do not want to better themselves. Finally, split from those who don't support your plans. If you do not roll away from these people, they will roll over you. If they don't roll with you then roll over them.

The first group of people that you should part ways with include: haters and thugs. A hater's purpose is to keep you from being successful. Haters hate, perhaps, because they can't do whatever it is that you are doing. Thugs are into so much nonsense that if you are involved with them you may get caught up in their nonsense. You run the risk of being robbed, incarcerated and/or murdered.

The next group of people you should get away from is the miserable unfortunates. A miserable unfortunate is a person who, more times than not, is in a bad mood and has a horrible attitude. This person is always involved in some unfortunate event and is constantly crying about how it is someone else's fault. These people are like magnets that attract all the unfortunate circumstances they can. All of these unfortunate events and circumstances become a schema in their mind that shapes their point of view, how they think about things and how they react to things. They become a catalyst for a negative unfortunate cycle of misery;

if you are not careful that cycle of misery and misfortune will rub off on you. Before you know it you are a miserable unfortunate who has lost the focus and desire to actively try and, ultimately, reach your goals. The danger with this group is: they subtly and unintentionally ruin those around them. Leave these people in their own misery, especially if you are trying to make achievements.

We all know people who are content in their current situation. They are content even if that situation is dismal. Contentment is displayed through their unwillingness to actively get up and at least attempt to better their circumstances. Never mind the people always crying about how they want to, or will, do better and how they hate their situation. If they aren't taking steps to better themselves, they are content where they are, regardless of their crying about it.

Anyone who isn't trying to better themselves isn't trying to aid you in bettering yourself. These individuals eventually turn into haters. On top of becoming a burden and making it twice as hard for you to handle your business they will sabotage your efforts. This is the bottom line: if a person isn't trying to do anything for himself, he can't and won't try and do anything for you except take and take from you and if that fails, he will hate and hate on you. Your best course of action is to roll on.

There was this guy in prison they called Graveyard. He had an extensive prison sentence and will likely die there. He is a sexual predator homosexual who has murdered in prison and has stabbed or attempted to murder countless others. He isn't trying to do anything to better himself or those around him. All he wants to do is have sex with men and smoke weed. He doesn't have any qualms about sabotaging the efforts of those around him who are trying to make it home. He has nothing to lose and doesn't care if you lose what you have. He is the epitome of someone who will roll over you if you don't roll away from him.

There are plenty of people in your lives who don't support your plans. You need to burn rubber on them. People who don't support your plans basically cast bad vibes which lead to you feeling unsure, indecisive and abnormal. All of these feelings keep you from doing what you are supposed to be doing.

I strongly believe that if you don't support the moves I am trying to make, then you are undermining them and there is no reason I should be around you. I refuse to let anyone deliberately or unintentionally mess up what I am doing.

HOW TO WIN: HAVE GAME

YOU WIN BY:

1. Getting away from people stopping you from succeeding

2. Getting away from those who aren't striving for success

3. Getting away from people who aren't supporting your plans

Humans are so vulnerable that the moods, attitudes, ways of thinking, behaving and the bad luck of those we hang around can become our own. If you happen to get snared by a miserable unfortunate you will either spend all your time in a bad mood crying about your circumstances, pointing the finger and engulfed in some bad situation. By the time you realize what's going on you will spend the rest of your time and energy trying to shake that unfortunate person. Miserable unfortunates need to be left in the dust. If they aren't dusted they will eventually roll over and flatten you with blame and misfortune.

People who refuse to better themselves can't assist you either. In fact, they often are haters whose hate surfaces when you are trying to be successful. I can recall when I was on the block selling dope many of my peers were content where they were and with what they had. When anyone from the hood started getting money and made the decision to have more than a high, a bottle and empty pockets those that were content began hating on them. I know plenty of people I considered my friends who wouldn't spend a dime with me unless they absolutely had to. Their actions indicated to me that they weren't trying to help me better myself or my situation. When I went to prison it became crystal clear that I should have moved on from many of the people I considered my friends. They weren't rolling with me they were just in my way.

If your friends aren't supporting your plans, implementing plans of their own, and aren't a happy fortunate, they are in your way and need to be rolled over or they will roll over you.

***

Chapter 3
Quit Rappin'

When you constantly run your mouth you are: exposing yourself in a variety of ways, hurting yourself and setting yourself up to be hurt. In addition, you may be hurting others, setting them up to be hurt and you are weakening your position. From my point of view it is extremely important to keep your mouth shut sometimes.

People who can't be quiet display their ignorance,

either their ignorance about the topic they keep speaking about or their ignorance about consideration: "Stage hogs" don't have consideration for those who may want to get a word in edge wise; nor do they have consideration for those who have heard enough.

In addition to exposing their ignorance, they also expose their lies, insecurities and lack of control. If a person is talking me to death in an attempt to convince me that something is true, chances are he is lying. For example, every guy in prison is the toughest, roughest in the land and many of them don't hesitate to tell the entire yard. They will hoot and holler and beat their chests. When someone calls their bluff their lie is exposed. Everyone finds out they had been telling lies the entire time. The hooting and hollering was a sign of insecurity. All the lies were attempts to cover up that insecurity. There was a guy who came from a prison called Westville to the maximum security prison where I was being housed. From day one he talked crap about how soft his new prison was compared to the one he left and how he would do this and do that. He did this every single day like he was a goon and everyone else at this new prison was soft. One night someone got tired of his rappin' and knocked four of his front teeth out. Needless to say he didn't respond like he said he would. He tucked his tail and from that day forward he didn't have anything else to say.

The downside to excessive rappin' is that everyone wants to try you and will support anyone who actually does. They all want to see if you walk like you talk; if you don't walk the walk they will be merciless.

Continuous rappin' is a sign of having no control. Imagine parents who have to constantly scream at their kids to keep or get them in check. The need to constantly yell shows their lack of control. Parents in control don't have to say much, if anything at all, to maintain or restore order. Many parents realize that if they have to repeatedly tell their kids the same thing over and over their control is limited, diminishing or nonexistent. A parent in control can say one phrase or give a simple look and the child will straighten up.

You are hurting yourself when you put your business out there: information that you volunteer during your rants can and will be used against you later. Friends will use the information to get themselves out of trouble or to shift attention away from themselves. Or they may tell your business without thinking they are doing anything wrong. Loved ones will use the information to hurt your feelings when they feel the need to.

In addition, excessive rappin' gets you kicked out of the information loop. Personally I go out of my way to keep things from those who can't seem to keep their mouths shut. They will put everything you told them out there sooner or later. If you walk into a room and everyone changes the subject or stops talking, you talk too much.

Friends are also hurt by all the talking. If you tell their business, it will be used by someone to hurt them somewhere down the road. If you are telling their business, the trust they have for you wanes and the bridge between you two will be burned.

People of power don't talk too much and are associated with silence. If you are in a position of power, you run the risk of weakening that position. Your position is weakened when subordinates begin subverting and disobeying your orders. In prison everyone knows the rules and for the most part is in compliance with the rules. However, if staff told us to do something, especially when we know the rule, we would go out of our way to undermine their position by purposely continuing to break the rule. They showed their weakness by trying to exercise their authority with words as opposed to action. We all knew the rules so we all knew we were breaking them; nothing needed to be said. The staff person should have just written us up and that would have sent a message that we could hear. People with power have already established the rules and the consequences for not following those rules. If their subordinates don't comply, there isn't anything to say, just consequences. Power comes from action not rappin'.

How to win: have game

You win by:

1. Speaking as little as possible, listening as much as possible

2. Action

Too much talk exposes your thoughts and feelings. Somewhere down the road it could hurt you if everyone has insight to what and how you think and feel. They can anticipate your moves, manipulate you and tell all of your business. A rapper loses his credibility, access to information and the trust of others. He also loses some of his power. If he says the wrong thing, he could lose it all. Stop rappin', words can't be taken back. Actions speak loud and clear. If you are tasked with maintaining order and enforcing rules utilize action to do so. In no time people will be in compliance and you won't have to say or do much.

***

Chapter 4
Respect the Game

Whatever game you enter know its ins and outs. This includes the rules and the other players. Do your due diligence so you won't come up short. Knowing the game, knowing its possible outcomes and being familiar with the nature of the players in the game is showing respect to the game.

Many of you get into a profession, hobby or a little something on the side without learning as much as you can about it. For example, dudes jump into the dope game not realizing all the downsides and are fascinated by the money and the status. They don't take into account that eventually they will be robbed, shorted, duped, sent to prison or murdered. They just jump in all willy-nilly and get their head knocked off. Then they cry about their misfortune and cut deals with the courts and throw their buddies to the wolves. They didn't respect the game nor did they play the game how it goes. Some games are dirty, either respect it by taking the good with the bad without crying or telling…or leave it alone.

Respecting the game holds true for every game. Take the publishing game for example. Distributors make about 60% of the cover price on a print book while the publisher makes 40% and the author makes between 7% and 15% of the cover price. Not to mention many of the books have to be given away as promotional tools. Those involved realize how the game goes and respect it. I know what I am getting into and I don't cry about it.

When I say respect the game, I mean learn as much about the game as you can and be sure you can live with the possible outcomes whether positive or negative. Be sure to read the fine print.

The players of the game need to be respected also. Some of you are guilty of getting involved with straight snakes that you mistakenly pegged as lames or stand-up dudes. Then you are left with a dumb look on your face and a bad taste in your mouth when you find out the truth.

I got involved with some dudes I thought adhered to the code of the streets. They ran around slanging dope, hitting licks (robberies) and packing pistols. One of them even shot me and the other drew down on me with a rifle on more than one occasion. When it was my turn to do the drawing down and the shooting they called the police and later testified against me. I blame myself for not respecting the game and doing my due diligence; if I had, I would've known they were weak cowards who would tell on their mommas to save their own hides. In circumstances where you don't know exactly who you're dealing with it is better to not tempt fate by finding out the hard way.

Respecting the game's players means finding out who he is, what he is about, what he will and will not do and anything else necessary to effectively and successfully deal with him. After you have the information you need and can deal with the possible consequences from dealing with that person then proceed. If you can't stand the penalties of dealing with a particular player of the game then move on.

HOW TO WIN: HAVE GAME

YOU WIN BY:

1. Respecting the game

2. Respecting the game's players

Respecting the game is learning and understanding what you are getting into. Armed with that information you can better play the game and be better prepared for the outcomes, the good and the bad. Similarly, respecting the players in the game involves learning and understanding who you are dealing with. With that knowledge you will be able to effectively deal with the player and the consequences of that interaction.

In prison White Supremacist gangs used to beat up on sex offenders. They didn't respect them on any level. There was one sex offender who would beat up the gang members if he was forced to. They would send one of their "probates" or the low man on the totem pole into the cell to jump on the sex offender and the sex offender would send them out with tinted windows (black eyes); this happens with the homosexuals in prison all the time. People think because they have their eyebrows arched and walk with a switch that they are soft. They approach them lacking respect and get beat up…bad. Respect the game and play it how it is meant to be played.

***

Chapter 5

Don't get knocked off your square

To certain schools of thought a square represents the truth. For this particular discussion a square represents a person's path to accomplishing his or her definite purpose or overall goal. You should stay on your path and not let haters knock you off that path. If you aren't on your square you are on a path that leads to folly and disaster as opposed to the truth.

When you are on your square all of your actions are focused on one thing. That one thing varies from individual to individual. That thing could be to graduate from college or bring an idea to fruition.

Squaring your actions allows you to stay true to your goal or definite purpose. Staying true requires the repudiation of many things around you that are being consumed by your peers including things like 20 inch rims, designer clothes and fast food. My momma stood on her square and raised two kids by herself, worked a full time job, a part time job during the holidays and went to school. She accomplished one of her goals by obtaining her Master's degree. She had to forgo many things young women her age enjoy: shopping, vacationing and whatever else. Everything she did was done in a manner that allowed her to accomplish her goals of raising her kids, making a living, owning a home, earning a degree and establishing the building blocks of wealth.

There are several tactics used to knock you off of

your square. They include: harassment, lies and objects like rims and clothes. When you are harassed you may become angry. Anger allows you to be undermined. Your anger keeps you from focusing on your goals and your actions aren't then directed toward reaching your goals. An angry mind acts without thought or control and displays a weakness that can be exploited. I have seen prison guards disrespect prisoners in an attempt to get them upset so they can have a reason to rough them up and take them to solitary confinement. Once in confinement the abuse can continue relatively unchecked especially if the prisoner doesn't have any loved ones on the street to call and get them to advocate on his behalf.

I was in a cell house with a young goofy looking kid from Anderson, Indiana. He was young, tall, with extremely big feet and an even bigger head which appeared larger because of the afro. Despite his appearance he was very smart, idealistic and defiant. Given his youth he was also impressionable. Over the course of his stay in the cell house he starting practicing Islam. As he got deeper into the practice he became more and more rebellious. He would always have it out with this portly, big belly sergeant. The sergeant was cool at times but if he didn't like you he could be a real asshole. We were on lockdown for some reason or another, and I saw the chubby cop arguing with the kid from Anderson through the hydraulic cell door. I am not sure what the young kid did to prompt the sergeant to slam the Koran down and step on it but that's what happened. A few days later we were off lockdown being herded to the chow hall. The Young kid and the sergeant fought over the incident. Needless to say the kid from Anderson ended up in the hole-solitary confinement. The sergeant couldn't wait to bait him in. The kid went for it. He undoubtedly suffered more abuses while in the hole at the hand of the portly cop.

Gewgaws, trinkets and nick-knacks like designer clothes and other things of greed are also used to knock you off your square. Instead of focusing on your business you get caught up in keeping up with the joneses by acquiring useless, impractical, expensive trinkets. On top of that you use resources to purchase things that could have been used to reach your goals.

There are several negative outcomes that result from falling off or getting knocked off your square. First, you obviously fail to reach your goals. Second, if your actions aren't square with your definite purpose, you run the risk of ending up somewhere totally unexpected. For me that place was prison. I was first knocked off my square trying to be like the joneses that happened to be thugs, gangsters and dope boyz. Then I let anger completely destroy my square and I ended up in prison for all of my twenties and more than half of my thirties.

How to Win: Have Game

You Win By:

1. Standing on the truth

2. Having both short and long term goals

To stay on your square you must first know the truth i.e. truth about yourself and about what it takes to reach your goal. The exact truth about you could be the subject of another book. However, once you find the truth you can maintain yourself control and keep your priorities in order. Once you find out the truth about yourself you won't be angered to a point you are easily undermined. When you learn the truth about what it takes to reach your goals little trinkets will be completely unable to interfere with you reaching your objective. To avoid getting knocked off my square by prison guards I began not caring about most trivial things; things that I knew would be used to push our buttons. I figured if it isn't going to impact my life when I am released, I shouldn't worry about it. For example, they would take our outside recreation time because the staff was having a bad day; I didn't trip because I knew not having rec that day wasn't going to play a role in me finding a job or a place to stay upon my release.

Stand on the truth and a set of goals and an overall goal. Don't let anyone knock you off that square. Self-control, delayed gratification and vision are tools that will allow you to remain perched on your square. If you fall and are knocked off, you can end up missing your goal and finding yourself in prison or poverty. Keep your action square and don't let haters knock you off.

***

Chapter 6

Man sharpens man

Proverbs 27:17 says: "Iron sharpens iron, so one man sharpens another." Social contact has a stimulating effect on our minds and personalities. There are many cons to being in isolation and many benefits to being socially active. No man or woman should isolate him or herself from society less he become dull.

A person in isolation is an easy target. When you

are isolated you don't know what's going on around you. If you aren't in the know, you become more susceptible to fall for all types of scams and plots. Imagine a country boy going to a big city where all types of schemes and scams are put over on victims, day in and day out. Because he has been isolated on a farm somewhere he isn't aware of the scams or the nature of city folk.

In addition to being a "don't know" (a person unaware of what is going on) isolation cuts you off from necessary information. I am reminded of slaves isolated on southwest plantations who didn't get the news that slavery ended a couple of years earlier. You need access to information to make accurate and effective decisions.

There are a few pros to being socially active. Like Solomon said, it makes you sharper; it helps you keep the proper perspective; it allows you to form alliances; it helps you stay relevant and it makes you more pleasant.

During my stint in the street life I had a friend that I would hang with each and every day all day. He was the slickest huckster I ever met. I had to watch his every move because he would get you for a quarter if you were slipping. The good thing about him was that he kept me sharp, alert and made me cynical. Hanging with him I was forced to pay attention to minor inconsistencies.

As I write this I am in prison. As a consequence my perspective as it relates to society is warped. I don't know how I will fit into society nor do I even know how to view society; this is a side effect of being isolated from society for nearly a decade and a half.

Without mingling and being a social person you lose the opportunity to build a network and alliances. Everyone I once knew in the free world is a thug. I basically isolated myself from normal law abiding citizens. Now I don't have any contacts that can help me get a job or be a reference on a job application. I can't call on anyone to have my back with regards to legitimate issues, outside of family.

I have been sequestered from society for so long I am irrelevant to my neighborhood, friends and family. I don't have any influence or say so in my community or my family. If your goal is to influence or sharpen people you cannot be isolated.

How to win: have game

You win by:

1. Interacting

2. Learning

By nature we are social beings. If we don't interact in a social capacity and setting we become socially awkward. Expose yourselves to social contact so that you can maneuver successfully in various social situations. You need to be able to move in and out of all types of social settings.

The point is, we learn from each other and it takes another person to help you step up your game. Others play a role in helping you recognize game, making optimal decisions and keeping you on your toes. If that isn't enough, contact with others helps you to view things properly, stay relevant and helps you learn to move through a room full of snakes, vultures and sharks. Without social contact you can't build your network or a team. Like the good book says, man not only helps you step up your game he helps you keep your game up, so interact and soak up as much game as you can and get it as sharp as you can.

***

Chapter 7
Do you

When you 'do you' you are being who you are, not who or what society wants you to be or says you are. To 'do you' you have to know who you are. Armed with knowledge of self and the will to have self-determination you can actually 'do you' or be who you want to be and do what you want to do.

During the course of your life, who you are is shaped and often determined by others. Your parents, friends and institutions such as schools and churches play a major role in shaping you. Society as a whole often determines who you are. If you grow up in a certain neighborhood or are part of a certain race, society will tell you that you are a gangster, a prep or something different all together.

In the area I grew up and lived in most of our likes, dislikes and things that made us who we are were already predetermined. For example, as a Black person I am told by friends and society that I like rap music, play basketball, wear baggy clothes, am hypersexual, violent and don't take care of my kids. While I was in prison I was supposed to strictly adhere to the prison culture and carry knives, traffic, get tattooed up and all types of crazy stuff. However, I did what I wanted and made it safely through prison without extending my stay or getting inked up. I have been ridiculed for listening to music other than rap and for wearing clothes that fit and I was talked about in prison for not being a follower of the prison's seemingly monolithic culture.

To 'do you' you need to forget about the ridicule and what your friends and family want you to be. You need to take control of your own self-image and identity.

One very important component of 'doing you' is self-awareness. We are all aware of ourselves to some extent. However, to take control of your identity you need to be aware of your individuality. As an individual you have the ability to consciously change the identity given to you by society, friends, family and institutions. An aware person knows that he or she has the freedom to shape and determine who she is, who she will be and what she wants to do. Self-awareness is equivalent to realizing that you have the power and the right to 'do you' which enables you to actually do just that.

How to Win: Have Game

You win by:

1. Being yourself

2. Setting yourself apart

Our culture is not a monolithic one. We all like different things, have different ideas and opinions, all of which make us individuals. Individuals do things that are unique to who he or she is. If you aren't 'doing you' then you are basically a peon who has relinquished his own self-determination and identity to someone else. You can't get your game past par if you can't be yourself. A pimp once told me that only tricks and whores care what others think about them and are the only ones who go out of their way to be what other people want them to be. My question is… "Who are you?"

***

Chapter 8

Have heart have money

Heart is strength, courage, will, guts and determination. When you have heart you are more likely to get what you ask for, overcome obstacles, take risks and create value. Without heart you become prey to those who sense you lack it. When I say money I am talking about wealth which includes: cash, land, businesses, education, experiences, allies, relationships, etc. Those with heart will have money.

People who lack courage don't ask for what they want or feel they deserve. Instead, they ask for what they think people will give them. Consequently, they end up with significantly less than they really wanted or felt they deserved, if they get anything at all. People with heart, on the other hand, are bold and audacious enough to ask for well over what they want or feel they deserve. They at least get what they want and sometimes much more. I've received many things that I never thought I would simply by being bold enough to ask. When you do ask, do it with daring, almost as a demand.

With heart comes the ability to overcome obstacles. The barrier known as doubt is removed permitting those with heart to continue on the road to their goals. Their determination forbids them from being halted by a lack of money, skill, time or uncertainty. With guts and enough sense to acquire the skills they lack, they prioritize and manage their time to reach their goals. Uncertainty is irrelevant because they know nearly everything is uncertain even tomorrow. Their heart keeps them moving forward in an effective and intelligent manner. Without heart things similar to doubt will keep you from accomplishing anything. You will most likely succumb to doubt instead of overcome it. I doubted that I would be able to complete a 39 year prison sentence with my sanity. However, I made up my mind that I would leave prison better than I came in. I had a substantial amount of resolve to "do me" and not fall in to the whole prison lifestyle. Although I am still in prison as I write I believe I am normal and in my case normalcy is money and it took heart to get it.

The "have hearts" take risk and reap rewards. Entrepreneurs and business owners put their 401Ks, IRAs, savings, credit, homes and families on the line to realize their dreams. They risked it all and have paid the cost to be the boss. They also get benefits like ownership and the right of inclusion and exclusion. They own all of the ideas and products their employees create on their property. They have the right to hire, not hire and fire whoever they want. In addition, they have access to multiple forms of wealth. They deserve that access because they had the heart to put everything on the line.

A person with heart is likely to be innovative. He will try new things, think in different ways and find new solutions to problems. In the world this is a valuable asset. Entire industries are created by someone who had the balls to think outside the box.

How to Win: Have Game

You Win By:

1. Overcoming doubt and uncertainty

2. Taking calculated risks

When you have heart you have money; you get what you have coming and you bulldoze through obstacles, primarily the impediments known as doubt and uncertainty. Heart allows you to take calculated risks that if not taken or seized will leave you on the path of mediocrity. The bosses have the heart; therefore they have the money. With their heart they add value to themselves, their organizations and society as a whole. They took a risk, perhaps even failed a few times, but ultimately won.

In prison, as in the wild, when you show that you are lacking heart predators come from all around to take advantage. Prison gets so bad that people who are normally prey turn into predators once they sense your heartlessness. Without heart all types of people, from those full of heart to the heartless, will run roughshod over you whether in or out of prison. If nothing else, heart will keep the jackals off your heels and that peace and security is as good as gold.

***

Chapter 9

If he aint hungry don't feed him

There are a couple of old sayings that go like this: "Don't cast your pearls before swine," "You can lead a horse to water but you can't make him drink," and "No good deed shall go unpunished." The way I see it these sayings are warnings not to feed anyone who is not truly hungry.

Elders in certain professions like pimping and masonry won't take apprentices unless they truly want to learn the profession. Often people don't want to learn the game; they just want to reap the benefits of the profession. They don't want to learn and follow the rules of the game. For example, they don't want to learn the psychology behind pimping or why patience and the best materials are used in the practicing of masonry.

Elders know that an apprentice who is not truly interested in learning the game will take shortcuts, do shady work and have the game all messed up. Elders realize what will happen if they feed a person game who isn't truly hungry for the game in its entirety. As a result they don't waste their time casting their pearls before the swine.

Elders also know that you can give the game to an apprentice but if he doesn't use it, all of his instruction was for naught. The elder would essentially have wasted his time. Time is something that can never be retrieved. Sometimes it is better not to waste your time leading a horse to water because if he is not thirsty he isn't going to drink.

How to win: have game

You win by:

1. Giving game only to the hungry

If you feed someone who isn't hungry, not only will he not eat he will not be grateful. This happens every day in life and in the streets. When I was hustling in the streets I would see one guy put his buddy on four or five times (give him a means to hustle usually by giving him drugs to sell). However, because his buddy wasn't hungry he didn't do anything but squander the helping hand. The guy putting his buddy on eventually realized that his friend was never going to be prosperous because he wasn't hungry. Once he made that realization he cut his buddy off. Instead of his buddy having gratitude for all the times his friend threw him a bone, and took losses doing so, he took issue with his friend not continuing to take out of his own mouth to feed him. As a show of thanks the guy who only wanted to help is robbed or killed by the buddy he gave a hand to- no good deed shall go unpunished.

In today's world where nobody wants to work for anything and expects things to be handed to them there is no appreciation. Instead, there are only black eyes given to the game, time being wasted and throats being cut. If you don't want to be a victim of black eyes, time loss and a cut throat, it is best to only give the game to, and break bread with, those who are truly hungry. The hungry will play the game how it goes, they will give back and ultimately represent and propagate the profession with respect.

***

CHAPTER 10
STICK TO THE SCRIPT

In this case the script is your plan- the plan you have created to reach your goal. When your goal is in your sights don't get distracted and deviate from it... stick to it!

To stay on track with a plan you must have a plan to begin with.

Your distant environments which may include the economy or laws are things that you can't control.

Your immediate environments, which may include your family or your business, may change as well. Changes in these environments will cause you to make changes to your blueprint. However, your plan, if effective, should not be disregarded. Parts of your plan may change but not the entire plan itself. You certainly don't want to abandon a strategy that is on the verge of goal attainment.

You may have worked hard for years implementing your plan and your goal is finally about to be realized then you are suddenly distracted. Distractions come in various forms like women, get rich quick opportunities and parties. You wait until the last stages of the script to switch it up. Flipping the script would be different if your plan was ineffective and failing but to deviate from the script when it is about to be realized is crazy.

When I got to prison my plan was to stay out of trouble and utilize my time to better myself, increase my knowledge base, gain skills, get a higher education and get my body right. My script entailed reading, studying, going to school, working a job, working out and staying away from all the nonsense that goes on in prison. After more than a decade in prison my plan has worked and I would be a fool to start playing dope dealer, trafficker, moonshiner and killer at this point. I created my script and I stuck to it. I stuck to it even though I was put in a position early in my prison stay where I really gave considerable thought to killing a couple of guys who jumped me. I had the knives, the anger, approval from the prison culture and the history to carry out my thought. However, my script was too important to deviate from it.

How to win: have game

You win by:

1. Creating a plan

2. Working your plan

I think we all need to write a script and stick to it as

long as it is effective. The closer you get to the finish line the more you need to focus on your goal and work your plan. I see guys get out of prison, stay on probation and parole for a long time, then wait until they are almost done with their obligation and jack it off by getting high on drugs or getting back in the dope game. If your plan is working, stick to it.

***

Chapter 11
Hully Gully

To reach your goals you may need to delay gratification or perhaps just do without. In fact, learning to do more with less allows you to do better. In addition, your goals will truly be appreciated upon reaching them when you have experienced doing without. Hully Gully, in this instance, means getting back to the basics and humbling yourself. Sometimes that's what it takes to be successful.

It has become a common practice to live way beyond your means and to have your priorities in disarray. Thanks to credit cards and loans you purchase things in advance that you can't afford. On top of that, you buy things you don't need and have no practicality. The result is financial enslavement and a blockade when it comes to reaching your goals.

Some goals that many people share are financial security, financial comfort and to be rich. To reach those goals you need to get back to the basics. You need to forget about buying all the worthless gewgaws that you think represent some sort of status. You may also have to do without all the things that represent impracticality so you can become owners of things that, not only make sense but, make money. Why purchase a $40,000 car on a $21,000 a year salary when you can put a down payment on a rental property that generates enough income to pay on the loan, property taxes, insurance, and repairs leaving a little money to put in your pocket?

If you learn to do without the things that really don't make sense and aren't really priorities you learn to become more efficient. You learn to make something out of what seems to be nothing and get greater use of what you have, that's hully gully. Your pattern of thinking becomes more efficient and you begin to seek ways to maximize your resources. Many companies and households in 2008-2009 were operating and living off debt and above their means. When the economy went down, those who delayed gratification and knew how to do more with what they could afford, not only survived, they flourished.

Until you have lived in a hully gully fashion with the minimum of things or without certain things all together you won't appreciate living the good life. You will take everything for granted. We all do it now. We take clean running water for granted along with school, air conditioning and our significant other. If these things are taken from you, you would immediately begin to appreciate them. Sometimes you might have to impose the hully gully lifestyle upon yourself, not only to reach your goals but to appreciate your goals once you get there.

How to win: have game

You win by:

1. Prioritizing

2. Working with what you have

All the dope boyz in my neighborhood wanted the money, cars and clothes right then and there. They prioritized these things over their freedom, safety and family. Most of the women and square dudes from my neighborhood went to school and/or work every day. They worked all sorts of jobs including fast food. They worked hard for what they wanted and went without many things and put their freedom, safety and family before money and clothes. Today me and the rest of the dope boyz are either in prison or have been to prison, are broke, can't find a job and don't have any assets. The chicks and the square dudes have all they need and most of what they want. They stuck to the basics and now enjoy the things from the top shelf.

In many situations you want things right now. You do things you have no business doing to get the things you want immediately; like committing crimes and borrowing money. You should just sit back, take a look at the things you really don't need and get rid of them or do without. This can help you get your priorities in order, make you more efficient and make your goals more obtainable. Plus, once you get to the top you can appreciate your success more and not take it for granted. Furthermore, once you reach your goal you can "stunt" harder than you can on a budget and borrowed money.

***

Chapter 13

Get your mind right

The phrase "get your mind right" has several connotations; the phrase can mean to set aside folly or get your priorities arranged properly. The phrase can also mean to consciously start using your mind. I also like to use the phrase to indicate the need to prepare mentally prior to carrying out your plans. If you don't have plans, then getting your mind right means formulating one.

Usually when we see youngsters engaged in a foolish undertaking we tell them to alter their course. We may have been there, done that and know the outcome is costly; therefore, we try to warn those involved in the folly. We also realize their thought process may be off or they wouldn't be acting a fool. If they were to get their mind right, they wouldn't be thinking about any nonsense let alone engaged in it.

Having been someone who needed to get his or her mind right you may know the thought process has to be warped if someone can't prioritize. For example, you can recognize a mind that isn't right when you see a person spend their rent money on a new outfit, some weed, entrance into the club and drinks. Obviously that person needs to get their mind right.

All of us at one point or another or in certain situations behave like automatons and just take orders and/or follow the crowd without thinking about what we are doing. We don't think about the possible outcomes of our actions. If we were to get our minds right, we could stop and think about what we are doing, why we are doing it and the consequences of our actions.

The conscious use of your mind can also mean to solve problems in new ways. When you come to an obstacle or a difficult situation you often abandon the endeavor or use old ways of overcoming it, ways that give you not so desirable, but satisfactory, results. To get optimal results you may need to use your mind and come up with a new way of getting over or around the obstacle.

Finally, getting your mind right includes preparation. Before you start executing your plan you must get ready mentally for the road ahead. In addition, you must factor in as many variables as possible, so no matter what happens you can execute your plan with a certain degree of success even if the plan needs to be modified. When I knew I was on the way to prison I had to do some mental preparation. How you get your mind right to do a 40 year sentence beats me but I did it. I tried to take into account and nullify everything that could happen in the joint that would keep me from executing my plan of getting out of prison safely and with more knowledge, wisdom and understanding.

HOW TO WIN: HAVE GAME

YOU WIN BY:

1. Focusing on your long term goal

2. Setting aside folly

3. Turning your desired reality into your actual reality

Setting goals is an aspect of getting your mind right. Moving toward achieving your goals is an aspect of getting your mind right. Without goals and a plan your mind isn't focused on a definite purpose. Instead, your mind is all over the place and probably has you in all types of folly and frivolous, insignificant situations like sitting on a park bench all day doing what amounts to nothing.

Get off the nonsense. Get your priorities in proper order. Start thinking, preparing, planning and goal setting. Also, use your mind to bring about the outcomes you desire. Your mind is a tool that can be utilized for your benefit as opposed to your detriment.

***

Chapter 12

Pride Comes Before the Fall

People become satisfied and complacent with their last achievements. Sometimes they even become arrogant. Their pride can lead them to stop learning and to overestimating their abilities. Prior to falling they are usually caught up in their pride.

Pride in this instance can be characterized as arrogance or conceit or more specifically the result of conceit, which can be complacency. People, upon accomplishing something successfully, stop. Instead of accomplishing more they rest on past successes and keep reminding us of them. They act as if they are owed constant continual praise and perks. They turn their noses up at people who haven't had equivalent successes. However, in today's market it is all about 'What have you done for me lately?' Those who have done things in the past are thrown by the wayside if they haven't done anything in the present. They are discarded even quicker if they are arrogant.

Pride also hinders their personal development. Once they reach a certain status or have achieved something significant they become too proud to learn something new and do new things. As a result of their unwillingness to continue to learn they become obsolete. Because of their past success and pride they incorrectly believe they are more capable than they really are. Once upon a time they probably were very capable, but we live in a fast paced world, a world where people are constantly improving their game and overtaking positions once held by a rising star that became complacent.

HOW TO WIN: HAVE GAME

YOU WIN BY:

1. Being humble

2. Being realistic

To avoid a down fall you should be humble and realistic. Don't "stunt" on those who haven't achieved what you have because they may surpass your achievements. Understand what you did yesterday is old news and so is what you know. New things and information are constantly hitting the market which makes it necessary for you to keep learning and achieving.

If you feel yourself becoming content, boastful and over confident, a fall may be close. Prior to me spending 14 years in prison I was running the streets, making a nice amount of money, carrying guns and shooting people. I felt invincible and no one could tell me anything. I didn't have any humility or a sense of reality. I was so out of control I was doing things bare faced with no regard for anything. I sometimes would wear a disguise that consisted of a dreadlock wig. However, I only wore it to buy myself time to get the jump on those who were familiar with me. For example, I was beefing with this kid who called his self J-Rock. He shot at me, I shot at him, he shot my car up, and I tried to kidnap him. I saw him sitting on a porch so I pulled in the alley came around the side of the house. He saw me coming but couldn't identify me immediately because of the wig. I was almost close enough to pounce on him when he recognized my face. Once he recognized it was me he leaped like a super hero off the porch and disappeared in thin air. I was out of control and I was eventually taken down. Pride always comes before the fall.

***

Chapter 14

You are only as strong as those under you allow you to be

A leader needs followers. If you sit at the top of the heap you must keep those under you happy. A boss's power comes from the people.

If you have no one following you, you aren't leading. To be an effective leader you need to have good followers. As a matter of fact great leaders have followers who are smarter than them.

If a leader doesn't have followers, he has no power. His power comes from those he leads. If his followers decide to do their job incompletely, ineffectively or incorrectly, the leader's power diminishes. If they decide to turn on him, his power is no more.

There were these prison gangs that were headed up by, nine times out of ten, punks. The leaders would be corrupt, overbearing and disrespectful to their peons. They acted tough and untouchable. Their subordinates got tired of the treatment, among other things, and essentially removed their leader from power. Usually this removal involves some violence. The former leader is exposed and left vulnerable. His tough untouchable act is uncovered, his true coward self is left standing alone and his power along with his former followers absconded leaving him weak. If he had a second chance, I bet he would do things very differently. His road from that point on is hard because all the people he pissed on while at the top are the ones he had to deal with when he fell.

Because your team can mutiny it is prudent to keep them happy. A happy team will work to make sure your power stays intact. Their happiness depends on it. However, if you think that only keeping them happy will keep you in power you are wrong. Those in search of power will offer your team happiness and other perks to get your power base. They won't offer it to you because they realize where your power comes from.

How to win: have game

You win by:

1. Choosing good followers

2. Taking care of your followers

Power comes from interconnectedness with your subordinates. You should never become corrupt or big headed nor should you mistreat your constituents; doing so will get you ousted by them.

Leaders are dethroned all the time. They were allowed to be removed from power by those under them. Make sure you pick the best followers because they are your power base. Respect them and look out for them and they will do the same for you. If you can't choose good followers create them. Your kids are your followers, teach them about followership and leadership. Instill everything you can in them so they can add value to you, themselves, your family and society.

Word of caution: beware of people trying to convince you of your own power. They are attempting to pump up your head so you can abuse your power making you vulnerable and then they can take your spot.

***

Chapter 15

Talk to the Head Not the Tail

If you are trying to accomplish something and you need aid from an organization or a group, it is best to talk directly with the decision maker. What sense does it make to talk to the peon or flunky? If there is a jackass in the middle of the road, don't attempt to move it by talking to its tail. Walk around to the other side and talk to the head. In addition, if you are combating a group or an organization, it is best to take out the head.

We go through life spending our time wrangling with non-key figures. Doing so is a waste of time, one of our most precious and finite resources. If we want results in a timely manner, we need to deal with the boss.

Bureaucracies, to me, represent a jackass and we are forced to deal with the tail end of the jackass. There are all types of barriers that we must go through to gain access to someone near the head and we still might not get the results we want. Jackasses are good at passing the buck and giving us the bureaucratic shuffle. This shuffle consists of everyone passing the blame onto the person above them, below them or next to them and sending us in circles. One person says talk to this person and then that person sends us back to the person we spoke with originally. Then that person sends us to another person who sends us back to the second person we spoke with until we say: "Forget it!"

You shouldn't get caught up in the shuffle you

should find a way to talk to the guy running the show. Getting to the head may be difficult but it's necessary that you be persistent, especially if you want the best results. I like to break the chain of command and go over subordinates so the next time they see me coming they automatically get it right.

Furthermore, if you are dealing with a group or organization with superior numbers, it would be too time consuming and futile to fight with each and every subordinate. The way to yield best results is to go straight for the head. When the head is taken out the body loses morale and the knowledge to function properly.

How to Win: Have Game

You Win By:

1. Not wasting your time

2. Dealing with decision makers

Whatever task you undertake it is best to shoot for

the stars; it doesn't make any sense to waddle in the mud. Your time is valuable and finite and it doesn't make any sense to attempt to get things done through people who have no decision making authority because all they are going to do is give you the run around. Dealing with the head allows you to get the job done the way it is supposed to and saves you plenty of time and headache.

Likewise, if you need to defeat an opponent who is organized and has many resources, you can't waste your time and resources wrestling with pawns. I watched a dude in the joint get all of his commissary stolen. He deduced that one guy from a click of ignorant youngsters stole it. He didn't do anything to the actual thief. However, he did fight with the leader of the group. After the fight he didn't have any more problems with the group. To have a better chance at dealing a significant blow to the superior force its best to go straight to the top. The subordinates of the group didn't want any problems with the guy they robbed and the head of the group didn't say anything when the robbery victim punched one of the subordinates in the mouth over the incident. Deal with the head not the tail.

***

SECTION II: GAME RECOGNIZES GAME

Chapter 16

Game recognizes game

People are always attempting to run game on us in an effort to separate us from our valuables or to put us in a trick bag. There are at least a couple of ways to avoid having game ran on you. For example, know the game or find out what is in it for the perpetrator of the game.

All sorts of scams and schemes are created for the purpose of stealing your money, valuables and identity. Scams and schemes are basically robbery without a gun; you don't realize you are being robbed until after the fact. Running game requires finesse as opposed to violence.

A trick bag is when someone gets you to do their dirty work; you don't have a clue that you are doing anything wrong and you will be left holding the bag. A simple trick bag would consist of me getting you to drive me to the store and I go in and rob the place, get back in your car and we drive off. You are basically the getaway driver and the only suspect because we used your car. In prison someone might borrow some dope from the dope man or some food from the store man. The borrower might give you some of the dope or some of the food. What he doesn't tell you is that he made it appear as if you were the sole borrower. You find out later when the dope man or the store man approaches you about the missed payment deadline, the astronomical interest you now owe and the threat against your safety if you miss another payment deadline.

If you are familiar with scams and schemes because you have been a victim or have practiced them, then you can recognize them when you see them. Sometimes you pay a high price to be able to "peep game". A more affordable price is to sit back and watch scammers work or heed the warnings of experts and previous victims.

Another way to avoid getting gamed is to do your due diligence. Before getting involved in someone else's proposals you need to ask questions, investigate and think critically. You need to find out what is in it for the other guy: find out whats his motivation behind trying to get you to accept his deal. Think about getting a loan from the bank. What is in it for them? If the loan is for a house, they get the house plus your equity if you don't pay. If you do pay on time until term, the bank gets what you borrowed plus a pretty penny in interest. Another example is dealing with landlords. They rent you property at high prices. Via your rent you pay off their loan, pay the property taxes, insurance, maintenance fees and you pay for their vacations. The bank and the landlord basically ran game on you, however, it is accepted and legal. If you do your due diligence and ask questions and make sense of what is really going on you can keep from being a victim of some clown running game. In our store robbery example you could have found out by asking questions whether the guy had money, what he was planning to buy, why he was rushing when he came out, where the stuff was he bought and possibly avoided being involved in a robbery.

HOW TO WIN: RECOGNIZE IT WHEN YOU SEE IT

YOU WIN BY:

1. Being able to identify game when it's in your face

2. Doing due diligence

The best way to keep game from being ran on you is to recognize it when you see it. If you know the game, you can "peep the game". If you can't peep the game then flush it out by asking questions and find out as much as you can. This will allow you to find the lies, inconsistencies and other clues that indicate something is amiss. You can also avoid people or entities that are known for questionable practices. You may also have to ask around about that person, which is an aspect of due diligence.

To recognize game when it's in your face takes a few things: experience, intelligence and gut. If you are used to running game you will be able to pick up on it when it is presented to you. You can also recognize it when you see it by using your intelligence: you can put two and two together. I had a buddy who almost got swindled by some foreigners. They led him to believe they could counterfeit money using some black paper, some kind of solution to soak it in and ten thousand dollars cash to duplicate. A person with intelligence can put two and two together and realize that it was a scheme. Fortunately these modern day alchemist didn't succeed in their scam. Finally, you can use your gut. If something feels wrong it probably is. Other parts of your being have a way of recognizing game when your experience and intelligence fails you.

***

Chapter 17

Don't be a stepping stone

In many instances if you are in certain positions, you are simply used by others so they can "come up". Unfortunately, those you help don't show any gratitude and often end up biting you in the butt. Being a helping stone is fine, but not a stepping stone.

Part of the nature of society and community is that we all use each other for one thing or another. You use teachers to learn. You use Bob to mow your lawn and you use Albertsons to make produce available for purchase. You even use people to improve your lot. The problem comes about when you start helping the undeserving and the ungrateful. They are the ones who use all of your resources, contacts and experience to make it to another level. Once they are on that other level they turn their backs on you.

There may be many reasons why they switch up when they get on top. Perhaps it is because you know how they got there and what their weaknesses are; you can expose them. Maybe they feel you may want a piece of their success and they are unwilling to break bread. In addition, it could be they know they don't deserve to be where they are and realize you only helped them because of your relationship; you have some type of power over them. To negate that power and not have to pay back what you did for them they burn the bridge that connects you two.

Whatever the reason for their ingratitude you

shouldn't have been a stepping stone to begin with. All you can do is put people up on game, give'em a little bit of it, not all of it, and let them make their own way. If they deserve to be on top, they will make it and you won't make an ungrateful enemy in the process.

One reason why you should never put a person on who is undeserving is because of how it will reflect on you. People who are deemed intelligent and are powerful know how to make good decisions. This includes helping people who are worthy and most likely more intelligent. When you help out people who are incompetent, lazy and out of place, you look: incompetent, lazy and out of place. As a result you weaken your position of power.

There is no boss who is successful who works with idiots and hires idiots because they are his friends or family. When you are "doing you" it is a must to use the best and brightest and not consistently be a stepping stone for the worst and the dullest; they will eventually destroy what you are trying to do.

How to Win: Recognize it When You See it

You Win By:

1. Being aware of game

2. Helping the deserving (see chapter 9)

It is not wise to help those who don't deserve it. Even though we are all users of someone or another you need to manage who uses you. You don't want to be a stepping stone for some clown who doesn't look back after using up all of your resources and good game and then burns his bridges. On top of that he may be a real life dunce in disguise who will be exposed and make you look like a dunce as well. You will forever be associated with all the mistakes he makes.

For you to reach your goals and maintain your image and position you need to use your game to recognize game. That is, you must be aware of those just using you to come up and those who aren't qualified.

I had a buddy who was in the dope game. What he did was attach himself to dudes who were in the streets making it happen. After a while he became associated with these dudes, the money they were making and the dope they were selling. One particular guy my buddy was associated with caught a Fed case and was locked up. Some of his old customers caught up with my buddy and wanted a kilogram of powder cocaine. They asked my buddy if he was still on. They obviously thought he was "slanging bricks" because of who my buddy was associated with. Of course, my buddy wasn't a Bird Man; he just kept his fronts up. In other words he knew how to appear to be something he wasn't. My buddy sold the dudes a fake kilogram.

The downside to this scenario was for the dude my buddy attached himself to who really did have the work. This dude is unwittingly connected to this scam and when the dudes who got the fake dope come across the unwitting dude my buddy attached himself to they may go at his head just like they will my buddy's if they ever catch up with him. You pay a price for dealing with incompetent, undeserving, idiot, snake, come up artists who use you as a stepping stone.

***

CHAPTER 18

MAKE SURE YOUR KNIFE ISN'T USED TO DO THE STABBING

In today's world everyone wants something for nothing. They want to achieve their goals without breaking a sweat. They take credit for the hard work of others and use someone to do the dirty work. We all need to be aware of the vultures ready to reap the rewards of our hard work and those who are more than willing to goad us into doing their dirty work.

It is recognized that vulturism (hovering over people and using them), plagiarism, or "swagger jacking" is a problem. That's why there are copyright and similar laws. People work hard to accomplish things only to have someone come along and take the credit and receive the reward for their work.

To be clear it is an accepted practice to take credit for the work of others and reap the rewards. Artists receive the credit and reward for songs they didn't produce or write. Business owners get the credit for all of the inventions created on their property along with a lump sum of the monetary reward. In both scenarios the individuals who worked hard creating the music and inventions are compensated but not like the performing artist or the business owner.

One of your goals should be to avoid being the workhorse whose work is appropriated by some vulture. Your other goal is to avoid being a fall guy, a diversion, or a sacrificial lamb. A common tactic used in prison by vultures consists of utilizing a fall guy. One way to utilize him is to send him at a correctional officer to determine if that officer is or would be a mule. If they are or willing to be a mule the fall guy would then get the officer to bring in a couple of packages. Then the vulture, usually a seasoned convict, takes over the mule, rides him until he or she is done and discards the fall guy. The fall guy put in all the work and incurred all of the risk only to have the vulture reap all of the benefit. The fall guy tested the water. If the officer wasn't willing to traffic contraband, the fall guy would have ended up in segregation, time added to his sentence and/or with an additional case. The vulture swooped in once most of the risk and work was complete.

How to Win: Recognize it When You See It

You Win By:

1. Being credited for your work

2. Recognizing when someone wants to take your credit

Don't be a sacrificial lamb. Don't allow your knife to be used in someone else's stabbing, figuratively or literally. Don't be the boyfriend who kills his mistress's husband. Don't take all the risk and put in all the work for someone else to reap all of the benefits (unless they are your kids).

Keep in mind that it is customary and smart to stand on the shoulders of those who came before us. You should make use of their wisdom, knowledge and works not only for your own good but for the good of others. Be sure to give credit where it is due. Life is too short to put in all the work yourself. Where would we be if each generation had to start from scratch?

You should be very mindful that there are people who will gladly use you to reach their goals. They will shamelessly peel you for all of your hard work and make it their own. Your task is to recognize this embezzlement and keep it from going down.

***

Chapter 19

Beware of the Herald's message

While I was heavy in the streets I was constantly being jacked up by the police. They would act as heralds: they would bring news that was supposed to be good, sort of like a heads up. For example, they would name snitches who just happened to be guys from the hood we hung with every day. However, these untruthful messages were used as seeds of doubt that would lead to turmoil, internal strife and snitching. The message was used to confuse and weaken. I would always be wary of any message brought by a "herald."

No one with an ounce of game will tell you what they really think, feel and plan to do. They monitor and control what they say to protect their weaknesses, true motives and obsessions. When the herald comes along and is telling you about his or someone else's plans, secrets or potential weaknesses you need to raise your brow in suspicion. Why would the police tell us who is helping them solve crimes?

Heralds use tactics to get you to divulge your secrets. They tell you something, usually a lie or some insignificant bit of information disguised as something very important to get you to reciprocate with some very significant information. The information that you give up will definitely be used against you somewhere down the road.

How to Win: Recognize It When You See It

You Win By:

1. Asking questions

2. Guarding your information

An idiot would have taken the police's information and believed it and assumed that the police were cool. Eventually down the line they would have given the police some real information in reciprocation.

Heralds bring messages of falsehoods and dissention. They use their messages to throw you off and to get you to put your business in their ear. You should recognize the games heralds play; think critically about all the information you encounter. Ask yourself what is the real reason why you are being given this information and whether it is factual. People don't tell you anything for no reason.

***

Chapter 20

Keep an eye on those who are doing too much

When a person is doing too much or is over the top, something is being concealed. Something is wrong. In fact, people use dramatic displays to distract you from their sins or wicked endeavors. Once you spot someone who is too far out there, watch them.

If it seems too good to be true, it most likely is. Imagine meeting a woman who is great. You hit it off from the start thinking she might be the one. Later you find out she has all types of issues. You didn't pick up on the issues because you were distracted by her big personality and her pristine resume.

There was a guy from the neighborhood who ended up doing a prison sentence in Kentucky. When he got out he came back to the hood and brought a story of how sweet it was in this little city. He told us how the dudes were getting so much money and how easy it would be to come up on tens of thousands of dollars. The story was too good to be true. He talked me and three other people into going to this small Kentucky town. We found ourselves in a situation that could have landed us in prison for a long time or could have gotten us killed. We did a home invasion in the middle of the night. We kicked the door down, not on the first; second; third; or fourth attempt. We fumble the entry which was loud and alerting. Once we entered the home the drug dealer and his family were wide awake, fortunately he didn't shoot, probably because we acted as if we were the police. We quickly found out that the story was bogus. The situation wasn't anything like he made it out to be. Looking back the story was too grandiose to be true anyway. Out of the tens of thousands of dollars he said was there, we netted about $2,500 dollars, before expenses.

How to win: Recognize it when you see it

You win by:

1. Believing that, if it is too good to be true it's false.

2. Not being taken in by falsehoods

Always be mindful that anyone who does too much, i.e. too much talking, too much hyping up of a story, too much drug use, too much use of grand names and too much use of spectacles is probably lying and is up to something.

For bogus plans to be accepted they are wrapped in

bright colors, loud noises, and given humongous names. So much is put into a ruse that there is no way you can't believe it isn't true. Like that sheriff in Arizona with his reality show. He would invite everyone in the county with warrants to a fake club or event. The event would seem so real with all of its bright lights, good music, large crowds and camera crews. The fugitives wouldn't have believed it was a set up if you told them. Even after they were cuffed and the Sherriff came out to inform them they were under arrest they didn't believe the event was staged. The Sherriff did way too much and the fugitives fell for it hook, line and sinker.

I fell for a similar ploy by my fresh out of prison homeboy. He told us that grand story of easy riches. He used us to carry out an act of revenge on the drug dealer that set him up and got him sent to prison. P.T. Barnum said; "When people expect 'something for nothing' they are sure to be cheated."

You must recognize game and not be taken in or distracted by displays of grandeur. If you do, the joke will most likely be on you.

***

Chapter 21

Alternatives used as deception

We all have or will encounter situations where someone will try to run game on us. One form of game that has many aspects consists of the employment of alternatives, choices or options. People give you a limited number of options all of which benefit them and/or harm you. People use the game of alternatives in blackmail, reverse psychology, the highlighted alternative technique and the bully blackmail technique.

The best way to avoid getting blackmailed is to never go in league with someone who is up to no good; if you are the one up to no good, never let anyone know. If someone tries to cut you in on their evil deeds or plans, decline the offer. What will happen if you accept? Later on down the road they will use it against you if you don't acquiesce to the option or options they give you. For example, I knew this guy in prison who had a correctional officer bringing in tobacco. The guy I knew made the mistake of letting people know what he was up to. These same people threatened to put an end to his operation when he didn't accept the options they gave him. By letting people know about his sins he decreased his options and increased theirs. The first chance they got to make demands on him they used his little secret to increase the likelihood that the demand was met.

Eventually, the people this guy let in the know threatened the correctional officer. They told him that if he didn't bring in contraband for them they would expose him to the administration. The officer no longer works in the Department of Corrections.

The most familiar technique used to get people to submit to their alternatives is known as reverse psychology. We usually use it on kids because we know they will resist us to the end. If we want them to do something, we present them with another alternative as if it is what we actually want them to do, but all the while we want them to the opposite. This technique is weak. However, if the child or person is very defiant they will go for it, if for no other reason than to defy what we want.

Another method used by gamesters is where they lay out several options but one is dressed up. The one dressed up appears to be the best alternative and coincidentally the one the gamester wants you to choose. If you recognize this method, the less likely you would be to playing into their hand.

The bully blackmail technique is as cold blooded as

it gets. The gamester positions himself strategically to control all the avenues. Once he has monopolized all of the vital resources he makes you an offer you can't refuse. If you refuse, it means your ruin. This tactic is used in the streets as well as the mainstream world. One example that comes from the mainstream world involves the credit card companies. You have a choice to either pay some high interest rate on your credit card or have your credit destroyed. Without credit you can't get a loan and in some cases a job.

The key to avoiding being bullied is to recognize when someone is trying to take control of the resources vital to your survival and stop them from becoming a monopoly even if it means buying up some of the resources. If you live on an island and your competitor is buying up all of the bridges and boats, he is going to own you very shortly. You won't be able to get supplies to or from the mainland without meeting his demands unless of course you bought a boat and a bridge.

HOW TO WIN: RECOGNIZE IT WHEN YOU SEE IT

YOU WIN BY:

1. Thinking beyond A and B

2. Dealing your own cards

The problem, in part, that allows gamesters to get over on you is that you associate choices, no matter how limited, with freedom. If you can choose between this and that, you feel that you are exercising your freedom. However, if you viewed freedom as having unlimited choices, you wouldn't be gamed by alternatives and allow yourself to be forced to choose between two evils.

Another part of the problem that leads you to be duped by alternatives is the fact that you often focus on the choices in your face and don't give any thought to what could be. When you are presented with A and B you focus on making a decision that consists of either A or B; you rarely think about C, D, E, or F. As a result of a limited focus you play with the cards you are dealt.

Recognize that A and B are not always good nor is the choice to choose between the two. Some alternatives you seem to be stuck with benefit the people who offered them… not you. Think beyond what they are offering. Avoid their alternatives and create your own. Deal your own cards. Don't play with the cards someone else has dealt you.

***

Chapter 22

Don't focus on the fire

Fire could be used to get your attention. If you solely focus on that fire you could miss what's going on behind you. During tough times it's important to really be on your toes.

At the turn of the century the U.S. declared war on terror. The fear of acts of terror had us all focused on Bin Laden, Muslims and the possibility of being attacked by al Qaeda. While this terrorist fire was raging the American people missed the implications of things like the Patriot Act and the assault on the constitution. Without thinking, the American people were willing to fork over their freedom in exchange for an illusion of safety.

The illustration above represents a fire, people focused on that fire and those same people are missing what is going on right under their noses.

In prison there was an incident that occurred over a shower. A black dude and a white dude got into it over a shower. They both began booting up (what a person does when he is getting ready for a fight in prison that usually means putting on your state boots). The booting up was followed by a stand-off with all the white dudes on one side and all the black dudes on the other. What I noticed was that most of the black dudes were focused on the commotion being spurred on by the initial participants and the white dudes immediately in front of them. Consequently, they failed to notice the other white dudes surrounding them.

Fortunately, the incident did not escalate. Nevertheless, the incident illustrates that focusing on the fire has the potential to be detrimental.

In situations where all types of commotion is going on it is wise to pay attention to what is going on all around you. Whenever an incident like what happened while I was at Wabash Valley Correctional Facility occurs, I like to watch what's happening away from the fire. By not focusing on the fire you begin to notice what is really going on and who is riding with who and you can gage their intentions; these things can save your life.

HOW TO WIN: RECOGNIZE IT WHEN YOU SEE IT

YOU WIN BY:

1. Doing whats instinctual-we generally move away from danger

2. Moving to a position where you can see the entire situation

It should be obvious that you would benefit from not falling for the banana in the tail pipe. However, we all do and we all do it often. We get caught up in, and distracted by, all types of things and fail to notice all sorts of other things. I was nearly knocked out in the club while paying attention to a confrontation right in front of me. I didn't notice the guy creeping up alongside of me until I was seeing stars and hearing whistles. Now I have a habit of trying to position myself where I can see everything that is going on especially when it looks as if a fire is about to begin.

People start fires purposely to draw your attention away from them so they can do whatever they have planned and catch you off guard. Recognize that a fire may be a ruse. Move away from it and peep what is really going on. If you don't, you may end up without your constitutional rights, seeing stars or dead.

***

Chapter 23

Beware of Ear Hustlers

An ear hustler is basically an eavesdropper who meddles in other people's conversations. Sometimes the information the ear hustler gets a hold of, from listening in on your conversations, can put you at a disadvantage. To keep your upper hand and your business to those you want to have it, be on the lookout for people hustling up on information by ear.

I am quite sure you have seen people behaving as if they aren't in your conversation by acting like they are immersed in their tasks or their thoughts. In reality they are listening to your every word. I am also certain that, that person has been you one time or another. I stay ear hustling.

Sometimes you may talk around people you don't think have a clue about what or who you are talking about. The opposite can be and sometimes is true. That person is not only tied to the situation but knows the other parties involved in the situation.

I've seen people ear hustle and find out about a stash and someone's esoteric plans. They ended up raiding that person's stash and the esoteric plan gets "popped off". Going through the jail and prison system I would hear people talking about everything. As a result I knew who had the tobacco, the drugs, cell phones, who had the work (drugs) in various cities and I even knew who had killed who in the city. Because people do so much talking unaware of who is listening and paying attention, many people have gotten knocked.

In jail people are always looking for a way out. Many people are awaiting trial for various crimes including murder. Ear hustlers listen and gather enough information about other people's cases so they can cut a deal with the prosecutor. For example, I knew one man on trial for murder. He was talking to one of his guys about his case in a holding tank. An ear hustler took what he heard, cut a deal and testified on the man running his mouth. Using what he had overheard he made it seem as if the crime was confessed to him. The guy doing the talking in the holding tank is now serving 75 years for murder and related crimes.

How to win: Recognize it when you see it

You win by:

1. Protecting information

2. Paying attention

If you aren't cautious of ear hustlers you give up one of your greatest advantages which is information. If you aren't in control of your information, you are not in control of the situation. There are some things you can't discuss when other people are around because there is a chance someone is listening. Ear hustlers are everywhere meddling, gossiping and trying to put two and two together.

Pay attention to who is around you; they may be hustling by ear.

***

Chapter 24

Watch the Moves of Those Watching Your Moves

There are people who sit back and watch the moves of others for various reasons. There are those who clearly have the jump on you and they let you go so they can study your moves. In these events you must watch the moves of those trying to "peep out" what you are up to and how you make your moves.

Have you ever seen a child watching his mother to

see what she is doing? If he finds that she is occupied he will carry out his mischievousness. Mothers pick up on their children watching them so they watch the watcher unbeknownst to the watcher, in this case the child, and are able to catch them in the act or thwart them.

Jack boyz (robbers) and other people up to no good are the ones who usually sit back and watch their victims. They learn the comings and goings of the people they watch. They learn their habits and are eventually able to determine a time when the victims are most vulnerable, that is when they strike. If you can "peep" those watching your moves you can, to some extent, defend yourself.

I remember when I was in high school I was selling weed. I noticed these two dudes were monitoring me at school. I didn't think anything of it at the time. Then I noticed them posted up outside of two different places I hung out. Late one night they approached me and acted as if they wanted to buy some weed. Prior to this night I had asked around about these two dudes because of their suspicious behavior and found out they had robbed another weed man. Naturally I assumed they were planning on getting me next. Fortunately, on the night they approached me I had already spotted them and had been watching their moves just as they had been watching mine. I was armed with a pistol and made it clear that I wasn't going to sell 22or give them any weed and that I knew what they were up to. Since I was able to watch their moves I avoided becoming a victim.

Jack boyz as well as police employ another tactic that you should be aware of. They can have you dead wood or red handed and simply let you go or act as if they didn't recognize that they caught you with your pants down. If you realize that you were caught slipping but are given a pass, watch out! The jack boyz probably want to find your stash spot and the whereabouts of those you are getting money with so they can get it all. The police are the same way. They will let you go because they realize you will commit more errors and lead them to bigger fish.

If you have ever sold dope to someone, immediately got stopped by the police and then were let go, I am sure and indictment followed. What happens is that the drug dealer sold dope to a CI or confidential informant. Since most drug dealers use some alias their real name and other information must be discovered so the police can charge the correct drug dealer; that's why the police stop the drug dealer and let them go. All they want is to know who the drug dealer really is. They let the drug dealer go on to sell more dope to the informant and the informant to continue setting up drug dealers. Once there is insurmountable evidence against the drug dealer and the informant is no longer valuable the indictments are handed down and the drug dealers are arrested.

I know plenty of people who have failed to "peep this move" and are in prison right now. A dude from around my way got played this way by the police. The police pretended to let him go after they caught him. However, they continued to watch him the entire time. Once they found out his studio was the stash spot they moved in and took him down with more severe charges than they would have had if they hadn't released him in the beginning.

HOW TO WIN: RECOGNIZE IT WHEN YOU SEE IT

YOU WIN BY:

1. Never assuming you got away with anything

2. Acting as if someone is on your heels

Gamesters don't pounce on their prey right away. They let them slip through the cracks and stalk them. When they find the prey's den not only do they eat the prey they eat their off spring as well. Whether you are a jacker or jackee you need to watch that dude watching you. If you know what he is planning, you can move in a manner that keeps him from knowing what you are up to, you can better protect yourself and it is possible to get the jump on him.

***

Chapter 25

Beware of offers you can't refuse

In the movies the Godfather makes offers that can't be refused. Either you take the offer or you get whacked. In the real world offers that seem to be ones that can't be turned down may not end in death but could have some negative consequences if accepted; therefore, I would think twice about agreeing to an offer you seem to be unable to refuse.

Some sales seem to be so good that you can't pass them up. You jump on sales to save money on things you weren't going to buy to begin with. Basically, you waste money by purchasing things you never intended to buy as opposed to saving money. In this case a sale is only an offer you can't refuse if the item is something you actually planned on buying.

In other situations an offer that sounds so good you can't turn it down could end up ruining your life if accepted. I have seen people offered hundreds or thousands of dollars for a ride across town or to stay in their house. One of my buddies and I were involved in a robbery. We ran in a drug dealer's house and got drugs and money, but not before shots were fired. Leaving the scene we got pulled over and got into a high speed chase. We got away, ditched the car and called someone to pick us up. We paid the person who picked us up a couple hundred dollars to take us back to the scene of the crime because we tossed the guns, money and drugs out of the car. The offer was too good to be refused. Who wouldn't accept a few hundred bucks for a 5 or 10 mile ride? The people I know who accepted a pretty penny for letting someone stay with them ended up with their doors kicked in.

HOW TO WIN: RECOGNIZE IT WHEN YOU SEE IT

YOU WIN BY:

1. Doing due diligence or…

2. Refusing what seems to be undeniable

Sometimes there is a reason why people offer killer deals: to lure you into their trap or what can amount to a trap. They use large amounts of money, gifts or whatever it is that will make you take the bait. So many dudes get caught slipping because they went off with some chick thinking they were going to get some sex but got robbed or killed instead.

If you are ever presented with an offer that you feel you can't pass up, do your due diligence. Find out why the offer is so good and try to determine all the possible negative outcomes. If you can stand the outcomes and the positives outweigh the negatives, accept the offer. However, always be cautious when presented with an offer that is too good to be true.

***

Chapter 26

Everybody Plays the Fool Sometimes

Some people may be downright fools but you must be cautious; some people are just acting. When a person peeps your moves they may play dumb so they can use your moves against you. Others play the fool so no one will suspect them, allowing them to make moves without suspicion. In addition, playing the role of the fool allows them to watch and learn the moves of others. Everybody plays the fool sometimes whether they are the fool or not.

When my little brother and I were kids we called ourselves trying to put one over on our momma. She would see us coming from a mile away. Instead of busting the two of us immediately she would let us go on with our deception. As soon as we thought we were about to get over she would let us know she knew what we were up to the entire time. We thought we were playing her, but we were being played the entire time. She played the role of the fool to play a pair of fools. The police are good at using this tactic. They will let criminals go on and on committing crimes and running criminal organizations then bust them down the road. They play the unsuspecting fool to get information, more suspects and longer terms.

When you are in the world playing for keeps you need to correctly determine who you are dealing with, an actual fool or someone playing a fool. If you enter the game horseplaying and underestimating your opponent, you may end up with the short end of the stick. Some people will sit back and act like they are oblivious, incapable, and downright stupid. This allows them to maneuver, go places others can't and get away with murder. This access allows them to put down major moves unsuspectingly. By the time you look up their plans will be fully executed right under your nose.

If you think someone is a fool or unable to grasp your moves and/or the implications of your moves, you will allow them to witness how you get down. Unbeknownst to you this person who has been given all access to your most intimate game not only grasps your moves and understands their implications he can pick up the flaws in your moves. To make matters worse he can take your moves, make them better and use them against you.

Kids are played by their parents like they are too young to understand certain things. However, kids are smart. They sit back and watch everything their parents do and say. They learn their parents moves and shock the hell out of their parents when they emulate them and put down what they learned by watching and listening.

HOW TO WIN: RECOGNIZE IT WHEN YOU SEE IT
YOU WIN BY:

1. Being safe not sorry

2. Limiting access

The point is, not everybody is a fool even though they may act like one. You need to be able to recognize game and determine if someone is a fool or just playing the role. Personally I assume everyone is filled with game as opposed to fools. I don't attempt to put moves down on people but I do try and keep an eye on those regarded as fools so I won't be surprised. I don't give access to people even if I believe I can talk or act over their head. Everybody plays the fool. Just make sure you aren't the fool being played.

***

Chapter 27

Peep Game: Everything is significant and has meaning

Life is like chess, to win you must realize you are playing a game. You must know the rules and you have to know how to play. When you learn to play you will realize that every move, even the pushing of a pawn, is significant and meaningful and that is "peeping game".

Life is basically a game every person is thrust into

upon birth. To be able to win at this game of life, as it is in chess, you must be able to think and conceptualize the outcomes of your moves. Chess players don't haphazardly move for the sake of moving. Neither should those playing the game of life. You make moves to reach a goal and to create a desired outcome.

Understanding that you are in the game of life is, for the most part, instinctive. However, it may be viewed differently or in more complex or serious terms. Have you ever said or heard someone say "this isn't a game; this is real life?" Real life is a high stakes game.

Unfortunately, the game of life has several sets of rules. You have rules the poor adhere to and a set the rich follow. The poor people aren't in the know; they have an incomplete rule book. The rich are privy to all the esoteric information and rules that allow them to transcend the regulations that hold the poor hostage. In addition, they are constantly rewriting the rules and creating, for themselves, loopholes that play a role in them constantly winning.

The good news is that if you peep their moves and constantly pay attention, you can learn some of their esoteric rules that have allowed them to continue to win. The ability to pick up on their moves comes from being aware that there is a game and knowing how to play it. When you learn why the pieces move the way they do, the implications of their moves and how to get the desired results from each move, you know how to play the game. There is more to the game than simply knowing how to move the pieces. People who know how to play don't make frivolous moves. In other words they don't do too many things just for the sake of doing them. Every action has a purpose.

When you have game-or the ability to play-you constantly ask yourself why did that person say that or why did she do that? What was she really saying when she said this or why are those two people associating with each other? You ask these questions because you realize that no move, whether it is an action, a statement, suggestion or inaction is unimportant.

There may be times when you can't make sense of things off the top. However, you should hold onto that information because it is like a puzzle piece. Alone the information is useless and meaningless but when you start gathering more pieces a clearer picture begins to form.

HOW TO WIN: RECOGNIZE IT WHEN YOU SEE IT

YOU WIN BY:

1. Seeing the dots

2. Connecting those dots

One day it seemed like our entire neighborhood was on the block "slanging drugs". The hood was jumping so hard everyone was making good money. A guy, who was nearly family and someone I looked up to, asked to use the gun he had previously pawned to me. I inquired why he needed it and told him that he would have to pay me what he owes and then he can have his gun. He ran some good game on me that consisted of him beefing with some dude on the other side of town. Being damn near family I felt obligated to not leave him defenseless. I agreed to let him use the gun. Later on that day I went to my house to get some more dope to sell. Out of the blue the guy whose gun I had popped up to retrieve it, I found it strange but didn't think too much of it at the time. I asked him for a ride back to the hood and he said he wasn't going that way and told me to stay in the house. I found that strange too. I went on about my business when something told me to look out the door. What I saw tripped me out because he was robbing his passenger at gun point. His passenger happened to be one of my best friends at the time. This guy who I looked at as family put his pieces on the board and started pushing his pawns. Before we realized what was going on we were checkmated. We failed to peep game and make sense out of several seemingly unrelated events. I remember my buddy "flossing" his fat wad of cash letting everyone know that he had a pocket full of money. I also remember the guy who was damn near family talking to my buddy prior to talking to me. All of the events were related and were the ground work for the robbery. To me this is proof that all of a person's actions are significant and culminate into at least one specific purpose. Friends and family will run game on you quicker than a stranger. This guy that robbed my buddy and played me was the one who put us in the game while we were still babies.

***

Chapter 28

Enemies are close

There are many people who know your secrets, strengths and weaknesses. In many situations these people could and often will end up your enemies. In light of this fact enemies are always close.

Family and friends are privy to many things about you that strangers or those identified as enemies aren't. As a result, unfortunately, they pose a possible realistic threat. These threats can manifest themselves in all aspects of life from the trivial to the detrimental. For example, a person close to you might tell something simple about you to others that is embarrassing or they could use things they know about you to plot your murder. There is an old saying that goes something like this: "If you want a good enemy, chose a friend." Friends become envious on a whim and turn against you; they basically work as spies and they act as parasites.

When your so called friend sees you 'coming up' he will eventually become jealous and in due course start to hate. Since he knows things about you no one else does he is more able to throw a monkey wrench in your "come up" or swipe your "come up" altogether. He can also destroy your good standing with others or at least plant the seeds of dissention that can fester and before long destroy your relationships.

In other situations your friend will deliberately compile vulnerable information about you so he can stay a step ahead, use it against you when the time is right and use it to his advantage. Obviously, this person isn't a friend. That is why you should constantly evaluate the nature of your relationships.

Parasitic friends attach themselves to people to make use of their resources and reach their own ends. These parasites use their host's knowledge, experience, reputation, contacts, money, hard work, power and other resources for their own cause. In some cases the parasites have their host put in all the work while they take all the credit and reap all the benefits.

To be honest only enemies will hate on you and be jealous of you. Only an enemy will collect secrets and other information about you for the purpose of hurting you or for their own ends. In fact, a friend won't use your secrets or weaknesses against you. Only an enemy will use you up, take credit and enjoy the rewards.

How to Win: Recognize It When You See It

You Win By:

1. Viewing everyone as an enemy

2. Treating them like friends

I've dealt with so many friends who were, in fact, enemies to the point that I now attribute enemy status to most people I deal with. I can recall when my house was broken into and close $10,000 in cash was stolen along with jewelry, collectables and various other valuables. Only a handful of people knew where I lived and they were my so-called friends. Most people are murdered by their friends who knew their financial situation and their habits.

I suggest you guard your secrets, hide your weaknesses and downplay your strengths so those close to you can't gauge your overall situation and use it to their advantage or to your disadvantage. Also, view everyone as a possible enemy because emotions like envy, jealousy, hate, confusion, anger, desperation, etc. can make people do things out of character. At the very least understand your relationships so you can deal appropriately and realistically with people. As unbelievable as it might sound we can go through life and never have a true friend but have many true enemies.

Although you may never have a friend in this world you still want to practice the golden rule and treat everyone how you want to be treated. Treat everyone like a friend regardless if they treat you like one or not.

***

Chapter 29

Watch Your First Step

It takes much energy to initiate an action. When you are the aggressor you are usually not in control. Making the first move has several other negative consequences; that is why you need to always watch your first step.

In concert with your fragility you have a limited amount of energy. By using your energy to go at the opposition you may be at a disadvantage. To keep with the fighter example, remember Ali and Foreman's rumble in the jungle? Ali used what he called the rope-a-dope. He sat back on the ropes for most of the fight while Foreman used up his energy attacking and being the aggressor, chasing his opponent. When Ali sensed that Foreman used up most of his energy he pounced and beat his opponent.

It takes less energy sometimes to make someone come to you under the terms you have set. Let them initiate the action while you conserve energy and keep your wits.

An aggressive person is not always in control when they are acting aggressively. He is usually caught up in his emotions, which are natural for people. The usual emotion associated with aggressiveness is anger. When you act out of anger you are not in control and are unable to see several moves ahead or the consequences of your actions.

Out of anger I kept coming at the clown who shot

me. My anger led me to disregard the consequences of carrying guns, shooting in public places, running in peoples' homes and doing all of this bare faced to a known informant. In addition, I was making one move after the other without thinking about them. I eventually ended up in prison.

When you are forced to make the first move you are pushed out of your element and you may very well be putting the gun to your own head. When an opponent baits you to come to him you will be venturing to unfamiliar hostile territory; in such a situation you are more likely to be nervous or scared resulting in rushed actions and costly mistakes.

Be careful not to shoot yourself in the head by making an erroneous move in response to your opponent's bait. The police use this tactic to get suspects to tell on themselves. They tell the suspect they have eye witness testimony along with other evidence and if they come clean now, they will be set free or get a fraction of the possible sentence.

Then they sit back and wait for the suspect to voluntarily tell on themselves, which usually happens

HOW TO WIN: RECOGNIZE IT WHEN YOU SEE IT

YOU WIN BY:

1. Laying the traps

2. Understanding

You have to understand that making the first move requires a large amount of useful energy. This is especially true when you are seemingly forced to make the first move. You become the aggressor who is out of control and lose your ability to plan and understand the long term implications of your moves.

Your emotions, most likely anger or greed, can blind you to what is really going on. You are lured off your turf into an unwelcoming environment where you are likely to make blundering moves.

It is better to lay the traps and have people come to you. You make the rules and do so in an environment you are comfortable in; where you can think clearly with planned deliberate moves. Realizing when you are being baited into moving first is also important. Many people try to get you out there first so they can take your temperature or see what you are on and how you will behave in certain situations.

When I was in prison there was an incident that I almost got caught up in. Some guys were putting a game of intimidation down on a young kid from their city. They were also trying to put a light weight game of intimidation down on me and one of the guys I hung with because we were alright with the young kid. However, they really didn't know who was riding with the young kid so they were reluctant to make any rash and blatant acts of intimidation. They suspected I was going to ride but they weren't sure. They tried on several occasions to get me to make the first move and expose my hand. They were trying to take my temperature; I had to watch my step. I played as if I was just an innocent bystander indifferent to all that was going on.

When you can recognize someone's attempt to dupe you into jumping out there you need to watch your first step. This is even truer when you can't ascertain whether you are being duped. In a situation where you can't make heads or tails of the situation get the other guy to make the first move.

***

Chapter 30

Pay attention to what's not being said

People generally only tell you what they want you to know and don't talk about the things they don't. However, much is said with non-verbal communication. Silence is a tool used by predators and one more reason why you need to make sense of what isn't being said.

We use spoken word to express to others what we

want them to believe about us and our views. In other words, we talk to disclose our points of view, beliefs and image. Being a cynic I believe we are constantly trying to convince people that we view things in a certain way, believe certain things and are a certain way when we may very well view, believe and act in a way that differs from what we lead people to believe.

This form of hypocrisy is seen at all levels of society. In the hood we talk about how we don't believe in snitching and view it in a negative light. In reality, many of us have snitched or will snitch. Self-preservation and self-interest are very powerful. In the ranks of government the leaders talk about how they don't believe in homosexuality, adultery and crime. However, they get caught in bathrooms and come out of the closet, cheat on their wives, take bribes, kickbacks and sell senate seats, among other things.

We all basically talk a good game for the purpose of

persuading and spinning people, adhering to political correctness and social norms even if political correctness and what is supposedly normal goes against what we truly believe.

Since the truth speaks for itself, it is important to listen to what isn't being said. The truth is rarely discussed. While a lie, on the other hand, must be made to seem true via all types of talking. If you resist a lie told to you, the teller of the lie will talk you to death until you believe his lie. If you believe his lie, he will still talk you to death to see how many more lies you will go for. The truth can be found in what has gone unsaid. You never hear your politicians talking about how they like to cheat on their wives or how they like to break the law for financial and political gain; however, apparently they do. No one, not even you, wants to talk about the things you don't want people to know.

Nonverbal communication also conveys the truth. When you are talking with someone you can learn various things from their nonverbal cues. You can learn if they like you or are interested in what you are talking about and if they disagree with your views. You can also learn about the perceived status between you and the person with whom you are speaking. You can pick up on the relational message in their speech.

People may say they are interested in what you are talking about and feel comfortable around you but their body language holds the real truth. Their physical distance, the direction they are positioned in and their facial expressions can tell you if what they are saying is true. Paralinguistics or tone of voice, pace, pitch and things that go beyond the spoken word along with nonverbal communication tell us about our relationship to whom we speak. You can tell by how someone speaks to you whether they respect you, if they think you are a clown, are scared of you or just really don't give two cents about you.

I try to pay attention to how someone talks to me

and what they aren't uttering then I couple it with what they are declaring to glean what they are actually saying.

Silence deserves attention because it usually precedes a whole lot of drama. Silence is used as a tool by predators to take down their prey. In the jungle when the predators stop roaring and growling they are on the prowl. Even in prison or the streets when the natives are quiet they are ready to move out. If you can't peep the silence, you may be the one who they are about to move out on.

If you are to be successful, you must not be lulled to sleep by the silence. When things are calm we fall into a false sense of security, lose our edge and aren't on our toes. Once we feel there is nothing to fear that is when we fall victim to the surprise attack.

While I was in prison I witnessed plenty of people who felt that everything was all good, calm and had nothing to worry about. While they were slipping they got hurt. Some lost their teeth. Some lost blood and nearly their lives.

Shelly G was an older black dude from Gary Indiana. He walked on a cane. His calf muscles atrophied for some reason limiting his mobility. The way he moved reminded me of Cotton on King of the Hill. He got into a fight (wrestling match), with a guy labeled a snitch. Shelly G isn't too mobile so it was to his advantage to wrestle. The snitch guy had his arm burnt in an assault at another prison for snitching and later attempted to tattoo over the burn. He was about the same height as Shelly, five foot seven or so, with braids that had reached their growth plateau. A few days passed after the wrestling fight and neither one of them said anything else to one another. The entire time Shelly G was plotting. As the snitch sat at a table playing cards, Shelly limped to the closet and grabbed a mop handle. He proceeded to limp upon the snitch and cracked him in the head. As he limped up on his victim the dorm got silent as they watched the entire assault. The victim jumped up injured and grabbed the lid to the trash can as a shield, ran to his cell and began boiling water to throw on Shelly. The fight turned into a circus. The guy labeled a snitch didn't listen to the silence. In fact he was lulled to sleep by it. I assume since Shelly didn't say anything or mention the fight the snitch thought it was over, WRONG!

How to win: Recognize it when you see it

You win by:

1. Being mindful

2. Listening to the silence

Your job is to be on your P's and Q's at all times even when things are uneventful and to make sense of the silence or what isn't being said so you don't fall for the okie-doke.

If I didn't know any better I would think that language was created to deceive, lie and spin people

(I don't know any better). We all talk a good game that is replete with lies and hypocrisy. Our truths lay dormant in the unsaid guarded with silence. We aren't in the habit of telling our truths as we are in trying to make people believe our lies. As a result you should listen to the silence so you can discover the truth.

You can "peep the game" contained in the nonverbal communication. Often the body reveals the truth that is being covered up by the spoken lies. In addition, how something is said or how someone speaks to you can tell you how they perceive you and the relationship you two have or the status you have in the relationship.

When silence is prevalent or there is an absence of the spoken word you need not fall into a trance. Before the storm there is the calm. If you don't want to get caught in the storm unprepared, you better recognize what that silence means and act accordingly. Predators-even the human variety-use silence to sneak up on their prey. If you can't recognize the absence of noise, chances are you are the prey. If you limit what you say and make use of tranquility and the silence, you are probably the predator.

Even what we wear, how we wear it, what we drive, the entertainment we consume, the furniture we own and other ordinary social artifacts communicate much information about ourselves. Pay attention to the signs you receive and the ones you give because there is a lot said when nothing is coming out of your mouth.

***

Conclusion

Game is wisdom. Game is protection. Game is wealth.

Game, in part, is the acquisition of knowledge using things like intelligence, insight, perception, acumen and good judgment. To really have game: knowledge must be understood, made sense of and applied, preferably in a righteous manner. Once knowledge is acquired and correctly understood and put to good use it becomes game or wisdom.

Game is protection in that it can keep you from the no good and save you from yourself. People in this world don't rest until they have done something they have no business doing. They use persuasive words and schemes that lead you astray. Game can protect you from these forked-tongue hucksters. Using game you can perceive their deceit and go the other way.

Sometimes we turn from advice and instruction because we are fools. Fools hate knowledge and the ways of a fool are right to him. However, if you have game it becomes mandatory to seek advice, instruction and to behave with prudence and discernment. Behaving in accordance with game keeps you out of harm's way and from making bad decisions and choices.

Game or wisdom is, as Solomon put it, more profitable than silver and has better return than gold. People can give you all the money in the world; however, it won't do you any good if you are a damn fool. First of all, you won't seek instruction so the cash is worthless. Second, a fool and his money will soon part. A fool with no game will turn his cash into trash by buying useless items or some iniquitous user of game will dupe him out of his loot every time.

For the above reasons your parents tried to give you the game or teach you to fish as opposed to giving you fish. If they gave you fish, that is the only time you would have been able to eat, but with game, you can eat whenever you want. Game allows you to go out and get it.

Game is to be sold and a fool won't buy. If it is told, it will be wasted because a fool won't take heed to the game. All parties involved will have their time wasted.

Some people and groups guard their game and the price to access it is astronomical. These groups realize that game is power, wealth and protection and they don't part with these things easily.

Hopefully, this book has shown you the value of wisdom or the acquisition, synthesis and application of knowledge. In addition, I attempted to give you game that will keep you from the traps of hucksters and deceivers while protecting you from your own foolishness.

Game is better than cash, gold or diamonds. With game you can not only get cash, gold or diamonds you can get power, peace and other things you value.

###

ABOUT THE AUTHOR

Edward Ball is the founder of Ball Team Enterprise LLC. He founded this company to help people extract lessons from their mistakes and the mistakes of others and use those lessons as personal and professional development tools. Through his eBooks and other informational material he aims to help people be the best they can be. He spent the last 15 years in prison and is an expert on making mistakes. After being sentenced to nearly 40 years in prison Mr. Ball earned two Bachelor's degrees, one in Liberal Arts-Human Interaction from Indiana State University and one in Organizational Management from Grace College. He extends the following offer to anyone with the ability and willingness to learn: Be better, do better…come learn with us, Ball Team Enterprise. I look forward to learning with you.

CONNECT WITH EDWARD

- Twitter: twitter.com/ballteamllc
- ballteamenterprise.com
- www.facebook.com/ballteamenterprise

***

ENJOY A SMALL EXCERPT FROM MY NEXT BOOK:

INTRODUCTION

Parents teach their kids to be thugs or not to be thugs. There are what I call sets of characteristics that are common among thugs just as there are characteristics common among people who aren't thugs. Parents, either knowingly or accidentally, teach their kids thug characteristics.

Back in the day parents respected their kids. They had enough respect for their kids to shelter them from certain things. I can recall my momma, aunts etc. using a different set of language and behaviors around us kids than they did with each other. For example, they didn't curse in front of us or do adult things in our presence. If we did hear them cursing we were meddling or we were in trouble. If we were meddling we would receive a lesson about staying in a child's place. Now-a-days parents don't hide a thing from their kids. They curse like sailors in front of them, have adult themed conversations in their presence, and engage in adult behaviors while they are around. Parents, by not giving their kids respect, teach them a characteristic common among thugs: disrespect! They may not have it in their mind to teach their kids to be disrespectful but that's what they are doing.

My book attempts to outline as many thug characteristics as I could think of. If parents can identify thug characteristics they can deliberately teach their kids not to be thugs; instead teaching them to be the best people they can be, now and in the future.

It is easy to inadvertently teach your kids to be thugs. For example, parents teach their kids' individualism or selfishness, they spoil their kids, they teach them about fairness, they don't teach them about money, about history, about a child's place or about their rights. What parents teach and fail to teach can become a petri dish where thug characteristics and ideologies are allowed to grow into a thug virus that infects their child.

Thugs are selfish and individualistic. Thugs want things quickly and easy just like a spoiled child. When a child who has been spoiled doesn't get what he wants he acts out and attempts to get what he desires using other methods. These methods may include stealing or throwing a tantrum. The child is practicing behavior that can become thuggery as the child gets older. Thugs only care about themselves and what they want. If it isn't given to them easily they go out and steal, sell drugs or throw a tantrum and rob someone. Do parents look at the possible negative outcomes of spoiling their children?

Probably not.

Thugs seem to have a hard time coming to realize that life isn't fair. Parents go out of their way to make sure their kids are being treated fairly. The concept of fairness is reinforced in schools, sports, and in the constitution. As we all know life is everything but fair. Living and believing that life is and should be fair only to be met with continuous unfairness can cause people to be angry, jealous, vengeful and many other things including criminal.

Thugs have an incorrect relationship with money because they weren't taught about money as children. Thugs allow money to make them. They make obtaining money their ultimate life goal, risking their freedom and wellbeing. In addition they use money to fund a cycle of poverty and thuggery.

Thugs repeat history because their parents don't teach them about history, well they may learn about George Washington and Martin Luther King. If a child and parent had an inkling of the tried and true plan that is in store for him if he turns thug he might think twice and the parents will work twice as hard to keep him or her from that route. Thugging isn't a new concept nor are the thug eradication plans.

Nowadays you see kids acting as if they are grown. You see it in their dress, their speech, and their behaviors. Parents have failed to outline, define, and allow kids to stay in a CHILD'S PLACE. Thugs are often children who don't know their place as a child and adults who don't know their place as citizens of a civil society.

Thugs do not know their rights. Many people have been cornered into thugging because they didn't know their legal, social or ethical principles of freedom and entitlement. One of my brothers was arrested and found guilty of possession because he didn't know his fourth amendment rights. Just as he has to obey the law so do the police as they carry out their job. If he would have known his rights he could have fought his case and won, however, because he was unfamiliar he allowed them to illegally search and seize his property, arrest him, and ultimately convict him. Many kids are having their rights violated and are being criminalized. Once they begin to understand and know their rights they can combat their criminalization and the criminalization of the areas they live and play.

Something as simple as teaching your kids about respect, consideration, the real world and not handing them everything they ask for can save them from the clutches of the thug life.

This book is about education: parents have to become educated about the characteristics of a thug so they can in turn better educate their children and increase the likely hood of raising a person who adds value to his/herself, their family and society as opposed to raising a thug. We can be accidentally setting our kids up to be a thug. I want to help you purposely set them up to be the best they can be.

Other Books by Edward Ball

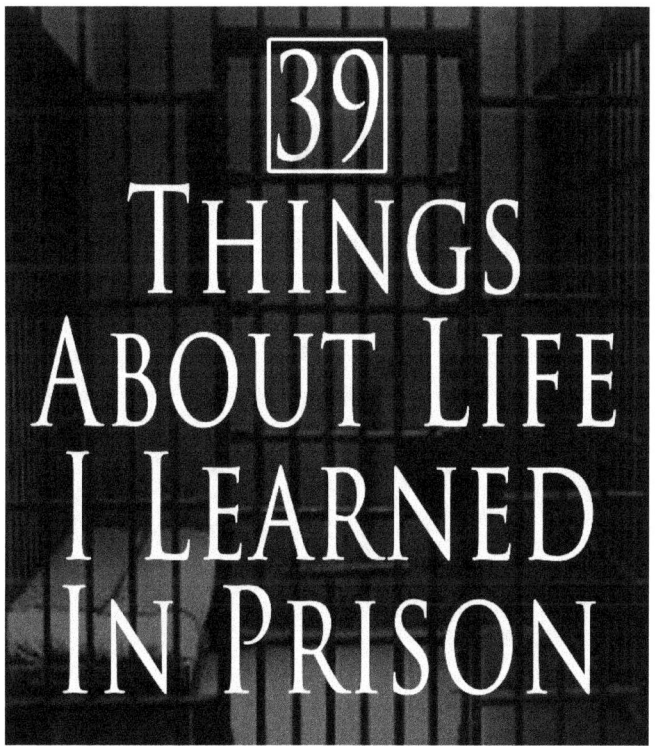

www.ingramcontent.com/pod-product-compliance
Lightning Source LLC
LaVergne TN
LVHW051520070426
835507LV00023B/3207